Strategic Outreach Roundtable
and Conference Report

THE EUROPEAN UNION'S COMMON

FOREIGN AND SECURITY POLICY:

CENTRAL ISSUES . . . KEY PLAYERS

Fraser Cameron
Roy Ginsberg
Josef Janning

With a Summary of Discussion by:
Stuart MacKintosh

Sponsored by
The Strategic Studies Institute,
The American Institute for Contemporary German Studies of the
The Johns Hopkins University
and
Delegation of the European Commission to the United States
Washington, DC

May 10, 1995

* * * * * * *

This document was edited by Thomas-Durell Young and William T. Johnsen of the Strategic Studies Institute; who, with Lily Gardner Feldman, served as organizers of this roundtable.

* * * * * * *

FOREWORD

The role of the European Union (EU) as a key international economic player is both highly developed and widely recognized. The Union's profile as an international political actor is much more limited, even though its activities are considerable. One of the principal objectives of the workshop on "The Common Foreign and Security Policy [CFSP] of the European Union: Germany's Dual Role as Architect and Constrictor" was to familiarize American policy and research communities with the realities of the structure, practice and limits of this policy initiative. The workshop, held on May 10, 1995, and sponsored by the American Institute for Contemporary German Studies, the U.S. Army War College, and the Delegation of the European Commission to the United States, also highlighted the special role Germany has played in the development of the CFSP, while considering, as well, the contributions of France and the United Kingdom.

The future course of the CFSP matters to the United States as it raises questions about the nature of sovereign decision making on the part of principal American allies. Will these allies increasingly come to the table with singular collective positions? Will such a development enhance European stability? Will greater European unity diminish U.S. influence? How will NATO accommodate the change? The resolution of these issues in the early years of the coming century will have a profound impact on U.S. European relations and gives added salience to this report.

The workshop involved presentations by Fraser Cameron (European Commission, Brussels), Roy Ginsberg (Skidmore College and Center for Strategic and International Studies), Josef Janning, (Forschungsgruppe Europa, Universität Mainz), whose papers are reproduced in this volume; commentary by Daniel Hamilton (U.S. Department of State), Philip Thomas (British Embassy), Lily Gardner Feldman (American Institute for Contemporary German Studies), Gerd Wagner (Embassy of the Federal Republic of Germany), Karen Donfried (Congressional Research Service), Pierre Buhler (Embassy of France); and extended discussion with the audience. Mr Stuart Mackintosh has provided a superb summary of the discussions.

We are pleased to provide these proceedings to encourage a greater understanding and appreciation of the European Union's evolving common foreign and security policy.

LILY GARDNER FELDMAN
American Institute for
   Contemporary German
   Studies

RICHARD H. WITHERSPOON
Colonel, U.S. Army
Director, Strategic Studies
   Institute

SUMMARY

Rapporteur: Mr. Stuart P. Mackintosh

Panel I-The Bureaucratic Politics of CFSP in the European Union: The Roles of Germany, France and Britain.

Since the signing of the Treaty on European Union (TEU), the European Union (EU) has undertaken a number of actions under the aegis of the Common Foreign and Security Policy (CFSP). An important development has been the ability to move from declaratory statements to operational actions.

The actions sanctioned have been broad in their scope, ranging from monitoring elections in Russia and South Africa, the provision of humanitarian aid in Bosnia, support for the Middle East Peace process, and launching the Stability Pact.

Most participants agreed that the Stability Pact has been modestly successful in mitigating ethnic and border disputes in Eastern Europe. The EU's involvement in the process implicitly stressed that those countries wishing to join the EU must take steps to rectify outstanding ethnic and border disputes. The recent treaty between Hungary and Slovakia (March 1995) may be indicative of future CFSP successes in this arena.

However, concern has been expressed over the lack of aims and objectives for the CFSP. The failure of the EU leadership to formulate broad principles of action has confused and disappointed external partners. Within the EU, this issue is seen as less important. Security policy is linked to member states' national interests, which often diverge. Therefore, a sudden enumeration of the aims of CFSP and an expansion of joint actions is considered unlikely. Those within the Union expect CFSP to evolve gradually.

Possible Inter-Governmental Conference (IGC) Changes to the CFSP Process.

The UK government appears adamant that the three pillars of the TEU (European Community, CFSP, Justice and Home Affairs) be maintained. Nevertheless, there are concerns over the need to improve policy making, organization, and implementation. The UK supports the Political Committee's central role on the CFSP process and may push for regularization and an increase in the number of Political Committee meetings. Support would be forthcoming for a strengthening of the Council of Ministers Secretariat.

British opposition to moves to provide an oversight role for the European Parliament, an interpretive role for the European Court of Justice (ECJ), or a right of initiative for the Commission, remain strong. As a small number of anti-European British members of Parliament appear to be controlling the British government's EU policy, it is unclear whether the UK position is sincere or being driven by domestic political necessity.

Some Member States believe it is important to change the voting system used for CFSP at the Council of Ministers. Others, including the British, are opposed to the use of Qualified Majority Voting (QMV) for CFSP matters. The consensus of conference participants was that the EU Council of Ministers appears reluctant to override vital national interests in the CFSP process because of the potential damage to EU unity.

It is not yet clear whether the 1996 IGC is likely to make incremental operational changes that will make CFSP work more effectively. If carefully phrased, the U.S. position on such changes could be a positive influence in shaping them.

Financing of the CFSP.

Conference participants disagreed over how accounting for national contributions for CFSP monies would be carried out. Some supported the German view that greater powers should be given to the European Parliament, while others took the Franco-British line that oversight should be retained at the Council of Ministers. Whatever the eventual formulation, the syphoning of monies from other priorities without a specific Community budget line may well be opposed by the European Parliament.

EU Enlargement.

Enlargement of the EU from its present 15 members to as many as 25 in the next century may cause problems but also provides opportunities and impetus for change in the institutional structure of the EU. Clearly, further enlargement will severely complicate the decisionmaking process of the EU which is already under stress. However, enlargement of the Union can spur institutional reform.

If the political will does not materialize, then enlargement could damage the CFSP, as the decision- making process will become even more convoluted and difficult. A possible short-term solution to this problem would require EU agreement that smaller groups of member states might act where broader agreement is not forthcoming.

The development of a multi-speed CFSP in the 1996 IGC would allow for this option.

U.S./EU Relations.

The Clinton Administration policy of supporting European integration and of championing joint EU/U.S. partnership is notable for its vigor in comparison to other recent administrations. U.S. efforts to coordinate action whenever the EU's CFSP allows will be maintained. Cooperation is being promoted through bi-annual summits and regular ministerial consultations, both formal and ad hoc.

There is growing Congressional concern over the apparent unwillingness of the EU to take more responsibility for security within Europe. This may be due to the difference between rhetoric which may be necessary to overcome internal inertia and the reality of what can reasonably be accomplished. The EU should refrain from claiming too much for the CFSP, which is still in its infancy. Rather, it must concentrate on achievable goals. Congress must be made more aware of the CFSP process and the Union must demonstrate that the EUROCORPS and the WEU can fit in a cooperative framework with NATO and the United States.

The U.S./EU relationship is dependent on effective joint action, and the impression that the U.S. is having to pursue actions alone could result in a backlash from Congress. Both the EU and the United States must avoid undue concen-tration on domestic issues to the detriment of their common goals. Partnership must be maintained even if the number of the U.S. forces based in Europe declines.

Currently the Clinton Administration, Senator Dole and Representative Gingrich support NATO. The Joint Chiefs of Staff still see the integrated military structure of NATO as essential. This shows strong support for NATO at present. Perhaps a degree of redefinition of the transatlantic relationship is needed, but exactly how this might be accomplished is unclear.

Panel II-The Bureaucratic Problems of the CFSP in the EU: The Roles of Germany, France and Britain.

A number of key differences exist in the new CFSP system. First, post-TEU there are no taboo areas. In the past, Council of Ministers meetings could not discuss issues with military implications. Second, the concept of joint action commits resources to particular policies within an agreed time frame. Third, CFSP opens up the defense dimension to a far greater degree than before.

The final text of the TEU articles regarding the CFSP was a compromise between the Community approach (eight states represented by Germany), and those in favor of a intergovernmental approach (four states, led by the UK). Because of the need for unanimity, the minority position triumphed.

France.

The French government opposes the Community approach and wishes to leave the CFSP pillar as an intergovernmental process. In approaching CFSP and the development of the Community, they perceive the option as either a "German Europe" or a "European Europe" with France continuing to be a pivotal player. Philosophical differences between France and Germany over the future political development of the EU will not stop the French government from maintaining the close Franco-German alliance. The alliance is the core of French foreign policy, and President Chirac is unlikely to alter this position.

Germany.

Germany is committed to the Community approach. It supports an increase in the powers of the European Parliament in the foreign policy sphere. The FRG also wants stronger Community institutions while accepting that such changes may not occur until after 1996. Deepening and strengthening of U.S./EU ties followed by a widening of the EU remain central to the Federal Republic's European policy.

Germany's position stresses NATO's preeminence in the European security architecture. The German adminis- tration wishes to see (viz. Kinkel's Chicago Council on Foreign Relations' speech) a stronger transatlantic relationship. Although there will not be direct U.S. involvement in the EU decisionmaking process, cooperation and coordination must be enhanced.

Chancellor Kohl, despite his belief in integration as opposed to intergovernmentalism, will continue to cooperate with the French to influence the EU agenda in areas where mutual interests coincide. Their cooperation in less contentious areas such as EMU will ensure their central role in the 1996 IGC and beyond. No other two member states have the critical mass to run the Community.

Britain.

A continued split in the British Conservative Party over their European policy will undermine the UK's influence in the IGC process.

The British government believes that the CFSP is too new a mechanism to consider altering it in the upcoming IGC. In particular, British Foreign Minister Douglas Hurd has rejected QMV in the Council of Ministers on CFSP.

Decisionmaking in the CFSP.

Dispute arose over the relative merits of decisions being taken in the Political Committee and Committee of Perma-nent Representatives (COREPER). Some conferees agreed that the Political Committees' role should be enhanced and that it would maintain its position at the core of CFSP decisionmaking.

Others pointed to COREPER as the natural place for CFSP decisionmaking. COREPER meets weekly and decides on multiple EU issues and is fully cognizant of Community dynamics. Doubts were expressed over the Political Committee's ability to understand the full range of EU concerns.

A suggested median was the relocation of the Political Committee to Brussels, with COREPER members advising. However, national foreign ministries may balk at such changes.

EU Enlargement and NATO: A Fundamental Disagreement.

Opinions differed over whether EU enlargement should come before NATO enlargement. Some conferees saw the need for NATO to expand first, given that the next EU enlargement will not occur until after the year 2000. Security guarantees for Central and Eastern Europe were seen as important for stability in the region; expanded NATO membership would underpin democratization.

Others disagreed, stressing the importance of the EU

relationship with Russia. Russian concerns over the expansion of NATO, resulting from domestic political pressure, ought to be recognized.

Preparations for EU enlargement are already underway. Gradual development of eastern European economies (through Association Agreements), and eventual membership of the EU, have not been opposed by Russia. Enlargement of the EU is a lengthy process, but prospective members are linked to the EU long before they actually join. This is apparent in the Visegrad countries which are aiming at membership by 2005. Preparations for EU enlargement engender stability in the whole region rather than undermining democratic forces in Russia. According to this thesis, rapid NATO enlargement could be extremely divisive within Europe and expose differing national interests and priorities within the Community.

U.S./EU Decisionmaking.

Conferees agreed on the necessity to improve the quality of intervention in each partner's decisionmaking process. How to accomplish this end was not agreed. That said, each side should establish mechanisms to ensure that the interests and concerns of the other are taken into account in advance of any foreign policy decisions. Failure to do so causes friction as was evident after the U.S. decision to impose sanctions on Iran.

WEU and the EU.

The U.S. Administration appears supportive of the development of the WEU as a partner either exterior to, or contained within, the institutions of the EU. While the latter is not on the immediate horizon, there is a growing acceptance by the elites in new member states that future membership of the WEU will be required.

The neutral status of new member states is therefore less troubling than in the past. Indeed they (Finland, Austria, Sweden) bring not only new financial resources for CFSP actions but also new perspectives on foreign policy development.

Europeans argue that care must be taken not to develop the WEU at the expense of U.S. support of security in Europe through NATO. This impression is contrary to the stated U.S. position which stresses a willingness to cooperate with the EU and WEU on security matters where possible. Rather U.S. concern rests on stopping duplicative efforts; e.g., is the EUROCORPS taking monies away from the NATO alliance, which could undermine support for the alliance?

It is important neither side of this debate overemphasize the capabilities of WEU or NATO. U.S. support for modest steps on collective defense should not be misconstrued as a major shift of support from NATO to WEU. Moreover, European support for WEU varies from country to country, and a consensus of opinion has not yet emerged among EU members.

Panel III-The Importance of CFSP for German Foreign Policy.

This discussion highlighted the centrality of CFSP in Germany's European policy. The discussion also stressed the FRG's wish to see CFSP support the EU's strategic role and future enlargement to the East.

German Motivations for Integration.

The German integrationist solution would support German interests while keeping her policy goals within the institutions of the EU. It also addresses the German public's reluctance over future unilateral actions on security and defense matters outside Germany's borders. A gradual building of the CFSP and defense arms of the Union would allow possible future German collaboration in intervention, peacemaking, and European defense solutions. The enthusiasm for this pillar of Maastricht is shown by the current German support for the EUROCORPS, C^3I, transport facilities, and the EU linkage with the WEU.

Given German elite's stress on CFSP development, a move to QMV on CFSP in the Council of Ministers is seen as desirable, perhaps also including a movement of certain areas of foreign policy competence to the Community level. This a far more radical step than contemplated by other current member states.

The obvious differences between Germany and France on CFSP development do not preclude continued collaboration. Instead a trade-off may occur between German CFSP aims and French objectives for EMU. Neither country can achieve its aims without the other. Germany might secure an integrated defense policy in return for other policy concessions. This more assertive German position on defense matters may indicate a change in the balance of power between France and Germany.

Variable Geometry or Concentric Circles and the CFSP.

The 1996 IGC may result in the development of further "variable geometry" or "concentric circles" within the EU. The outer circle characterizes those countries with partnership agreements with the EU; the second, full EU members; and a third, core group who "opt in" to greater CFSP solidarity. Such a multilayered Community will be resisted by certain member states, but the decision of France and Germany on these formulations will be crucial to the outcome.

In the opinion of the French, successful enhancement of CFSP will work if it conforms to subsidiarity, at the same time allowing increased cooperation between willing states. Enhanced solidarity of the type envisaged in the concentric circles would allow faster development of CFSP.

Whether this new CFSP is a core group or a fourth pillar in the Community structure is less important than decisions over the institutional allocation of power in an enhanced CFSP. Regardless, it is an area which will create conflicts of interest.

Finally, participants stressed the importance of considering CFSP as only one part of the Union's external policy options. Security policy can no longer be divorced from economic policy. The latter can be used to achieve aims contained in the former.

THE BUREAUCRATIC POLITICS OF CFSP IN THE EUROPEAN UNION: THE ROLES OF GERMANY, FRANCE AND BRITAIN[1]

Fraser Cameron

Introduction.

These are confusing times for anyone trying to work out whether the European Union (EU) has any prospect of developing a common foreign and security policy (CFSP) worth the name. When the CFSP was established, it was in answer to a range of internal and external challenges. *Internally*, the completion of the Single Market and the drive toward economic and monetary union (EMU) necessitated corresponding moves towards Political Union, of which CFSP was a central element. *Externally*, Europe was expected to use its economic weight to achieve more political influence and ensure stability around its borders.

The 1991 Maastricht negotiations to establish the Treaty on European Union (TEU) took place in the midst of a geopolitical earthquake which hit Europe following the collapse of communism and failed to take into account, let alone attempt to meet, the enormous challenges posed by the unification of Germany, the sweeping changes in central and eastern Europe, and the disintegration of the Soviet Union. There were high expectations for the CFSP which superseded the previous light framework of European Political Cooperation (EPC). The European Council became directly involved, not only through the single institutional structure, but also as the body to issue mandates for joint. The views expressed are personal and do not commit the European Commission in any way.> actions. Title V included a number of improvements, such as the ending of taboo areas (one could now discuss issues having military implications), the provision for joint actions (Article J.3), and even for majority voting, albeit only on the implementation of joint actions, common positions (Article J.2) and the inclusion of security and defense (Article J.4) with the WEU designated "an integral part of the development of the European Union."

The final text of the Treaty represented a compromise between the advocates of a community approach (8 member states led by Germany) and those in favor of an inter-governmental approach (4 member states led by the UK and France). Given the need for unanimity at the IGC, the minority in favor of an intergovernmental approach were able to carry the day. A pillar structure was thus established which involved different arrangements for CFSP (and the third pillar covering Justice/Internal Affairs) than used for the first, or Community pillar. Jacques Delors considered the changes a recipe for confusion. Regrettably, his forecast has been proved all too accurate with numerous EU disputes over competencies between the different pillars.

The treaty text also papered over a dispute between the so-called Atlanticists and Europeans as regards the question of common defense. It was agreed to review the defense aspect and the institutional working of CFSP at the IGC in 1996.

Since Maastricht, three countries (Austria, Sweden and Finland), one of which has a 1200 km border with Russia, have joined the EU. It is likely that by the Cannes European Council in June there will be *ten associated states* in central and eastern Europe-all of whom have made it crystal clear that EU membership is a top priority. Turkey, Switzerland, Cyprus and Malta all still have applications on the table. In short, it is not difficult to imagine a 25-30 strong EU within the next decade.

This paper seeks to examine the CFSP in operation, discusses its weaknesses, suggests some areas for improvement and assesses the attitudes of Germany, France and Britain both to current arrangements and likely future proposals.

The CFSP in Operation.

Although the CFSP only has been in operation for less than 18 months, it has been widely criticized for its cumbersome procedures and lack of effectiveness. Kissinger's question in the early 1970s, "Who do we call in Europe?", remains unanswered. An earnest debate on how to improve the CFSP is gathering pace at a time when the EU's three biggest diplomatic players-Germany, France and Britain-are struggling hard to maintain a minimum of consensus over some of the biggest foreign policy challenges they face, such as the conflict in former Yugoslavia. Throughout much of the Bosnian drama, Germany has shown more sympathy with U.S. attitudes than with those of her EU partners. On policy toward Iraq, the alignment is different: London backs the U.S. tough stance, while France and Germany take a softer line. In respect to Iran, however, the Europeans are united in their opposition to the U.S. big stick approach.

These difficulties do not mean that the quest for a more effective CFSP should be abandoned. The main argument in favor of such a policy is quite simple: in most parts of the world, the EU will either speak with one voice, or its voice will not be heard at all. This also applies in Washington where U.S. officials, unlike the situation in 1991, have made clear their preference for a single European voice in international affairs. Indeed the Clinton administration is perhaps the strongest supporter of the need to create an European Security and Defense Identity (ESDI). Discussions on how to establish ESDI and the corresponding Combined Joint Task Force (CJTF) are currently taking place between WEU and NATO but it is unlikely that there will be any agreement on the details until the new French President has reviewed French security policy, and perhaps not before the outcome of next year's intergovernmental conference (IGC), at which a review of CFSP in operation and the defense dimension will be high on the agenda.

An initial assessment of the CFSP in operation is *not* very encouraging. Certainly there has been a vast increase in the number of meetings and a considerable reorganization of the various bureaucracies involved. The European Commission has established a separate Directorate General (DG1A) to cover CFSP, under the mixed authority of President Santer and Hans van den Broek; the Council has also established a new Directorate to deal with CFSP, headed by a British diplomat; while the WEU's Secretariat has moved from London to Brussels.

Since the TEU came into operation on November 1, 1993, the EU has agreed to a number of Joint Actions including:

- monitoring elections in Russia and in South Africa;

- providing humanitarian assistance in former Yugoslavia and establishing an administration for Mostar;

- supporting the Middle East Peace Process;

- lobbying for the extension of the NPT;

- agreeing to export guidelines for the use of dual use goods; and,

- promoting the Stability Pact to tackle problems concerned with borders/minorities in central and eastern Europe.

In addition to these "joint actions," a number of "common positions" (i.e., alignment of policies but not necessarily taking action together or committing resources) have been adopted on

Commission (disputes over the interpretation of "fully associated") and the form of the Union's external representation. Some Foreign Ministers holding the Presidency seem to have difficulty in making any distinction between representing a national position and an EU position. Furthermore, in many capitals outside Europe, the presence of the EU is conspicuous by its absence.

The Need for Improvements.

Given the prospect of a substantially enlarged Union in the not too distant future, an increasingly unstable international environment and encouragement from the U.S. to achieve a credible CFSP, it is imperative that the IGC results in an enhanced and effective CFSP. Although an absence of political will cannot itself be tackled through procedural improvements, such improvements, taken together, may reinforce the sense of common objectives and common interests, leading to a greater propensity to act together. Some proposals already on the table include:

Policy Planning. An awareness of common European interests can be increased by partially pooling the Union's capacity for policy analysis. This already takes place to some extent through the exchange of information on the EU telegraphic COREU network and by joint meetings of policy planning staff from the member states and the Union's institutions. Such cooperation is limited, however, and could be enhanced by establishing a joint structure for the evaluation of information, policy analysis and preparation of policy actions. One proposal is that this body should be a joint Commission-Council body, which would maintain close links with WEU and which could be enhanced by officials on detachment from member states and perhaps also academic specialists.

Policy Objectives and Priorities. The TEU and recent European Council conclusions provide only a general guide to the objectives and priorities of the CFSP. This hampers decisive action when situations arise requiring preventive diplomacy, crisis management or conflict resolution. The Union's capacity for action could be enhanced if it were to produce an annual report and guidelines for the Union's external relations. This could be a task for the policy planners mentioned above. The Council would then debate the guidelines, having first sought the views of the European Parliament. After Parliament had given its opinion, the guidelines could be reviewed by the Council and then transmitted to the European Council for approval. These guidelines would then create the parameters for EU decisionmaking on external policy during the course of the year.

Decisionmaking. Until now unanimity has been required for joint action under the CFSP although, in principle, the Treaty allows for decision by qualified majority on the details of implementing measures. This means that the Union's capacity for action can be limited by the reluctance of a single member state. While respecting national prerogatives on matters of vital interest in fundamental areas of foreign and security policy, decisionmaking rules could be changed to permit member states wishing to take action together, to do so within the framework of the treaty. Such actions would only be agreed if they fell within the broad guidelines approved by the European Council. Other member states, though not necessarily participating directly, would not be able to prevent the joint action from taking place. Indeed, such an approach, which will be even more desirable in an enlarged EU, finds its origin in the declaration attached to the Treaty concerning the CFSP, which aims at preventing the blockage of unanimity where a qualified majority exists. Obviously there needs to be a reform of the voting system to allow for a greater correlation with population size. Ministers also need to discuss issues working from a similar information basis; and the CFSP infrastructure (Political Committee, European Corre- spondents, Planners, Working Groups) must prepare options for ministerial decision.

Finance. The Union would lose effectiveness and credibility if such actions were held up, as in the past, because of difficulty in mobilizing the necessary resources. It is thus essential that the Council determine the modalities of financing whenever it decides on a joint action. Normally, financing through the Union's budget is to be preferred to national contributions for reasons of coherence and transparency. The CFSP budget line should receive an adequate initial allocation, estimated on the basis of past experience, through the annual budgetary procedure. Finance from this line should be mobilized quickly when the need arises. It may also be necessary to mobilize resources from relevant budget lines for Community activities in support of joint actions, as has occurred hitherto. Depending on the evolution of needs under the CFSP, it may be necessary to revise the financial perspectives to make sufficient resources available to ensure that the Union's external policy is fully effective.

External Representation. Under the treaty, the Presidency was given an increased role as regards external representation of the Union. The Commission was also tasked with ensuring coherence between the pillars. It is doubtful, however, whether the present 6-monthly rotation system can be maintained in an enlarged Union.

It is difficult to imagine Malta running the Presidency. And a troika of Latvia, Lithuania and Luxembourg stretches the imagination. Even with adjustments to the troika rotation, one cannot escape the fact that future enlargements will concern mainly small and indeed very small states. The solution is not a directoire nor a new body to oversee CFSP but rather a strengthening of the Community institutions.[2] This is the logical path which two senior officials from the Auswärtiges Amt correctly identified in the article in the *Frankfurter Allgemeine* on 30 March 1995.

As far as the Commission's role is concerned, it is fully associated with the implementation of the CFSP and has the right of initiative, a right shared with the Presidency and other member states. The Commission is uniquely well placed to provide the European perspective and has demonstrated this in the past year by preparing numerous, well-received papers covering EU policy toward central and eastern Europe, Russia, Ukraine, the Baltic states, the Mediterranean, Asia, Japan, Common Market of the South (MERCOSUR), etc. Member states inevitably approach problems from a national perspective while the Council has neither the experience nor the critical mass of officials to undertake new tasks in CFSP.

Furthermore, the Commission is an institution which provides continuity through changing presidencies and troikas. On the whole, the Presidency-Commission form of external representation (e.g., for démarches) is more coherent than the somewhat unwieldy troika formula. In the longer term, under the impact of enlargement, there is a strong case for the Commission to act, under a Council mandate, in the whole range of external policies. One could envisage a senior Vice-President for foreign affairs (rather like Sir Leon Brittan's role on the trade side) who would speak for, and represent the Union in areas agreed upon by the Council. An alternative proposal which has been suggested would involve an independent CFSP Secretariat, roughly modelled on the NATO example.

Security and Defense.

The Maastricht Treaty provides for the possibility of a common defense policy, which might in time lead to a common defense. In the past two years little progress has been made toward achieving this goal. The relationship between the WEU and NATO is indeed more highly developed than that between the WEU and the EU.

The relationship between the WEU, which is, according to the

Treaty, "an integral part of the development of the European Union," the EU itself, and NATO, which is today the principal framework for ensuring the defense of its members, is of course a sensitive area and the IGC will wish to consider various options: whether to maintain the status quo, whether to enhance the capability of the WEU but leave it outside the EU, or whether to bring it within the single institutional framework of the EU, albeit perhaps as a separate pillar. At present it is difficult to envisage agreement to bring the WEU into the EU framework in 1996, but it is important not to relinquish this as an EU goal. Obviously the extent of any changes will depend on outside developments, particularly in Russia and the United States, as well as EU internal dynamics.

While working toward a consensus on the future division of responsibilities between the WEU and NATO, the Union is gradually attempting to create a European intervention force, under the WEU umbrella, for use in the framework of joint actions under the CFSP. There is increasing awareness that one of the most glaring lessons of the Yugoslav crisis is that the lack of a credible military instrument severely handicaps diplomatic efforts.

One of the most significant changes since 1991 has been the change in the U.S. position as regards ESDI. Indeed there is a strong argument that the future health of the transatlantic relationship depends on the EU developing an effective CFSP, including a defense dimension. Talk of a new transatlantic treaty is premature, however, at least until the Union demonstrates that it is capable of an effective foreign and security policy.

The German Position.

The Germans have consistently been one of the strongest supporters of a *communautaire* approach to CFSP. At Maastricht they were not in favor of establishing separate pillars, but could not persuade the British or French to change their views. The Germans have continued to snipe at the British for their negative attitude towards Europe in general and CFSP/Bosnia in particular. Although they have not yet defined their position for the IGC, German spokesmen have stated that they will attempt to secure a greater community involvement in CFSP.

During their Presidency (July-December 1994), the Germans did not seek to introduce any new initiatives under CFSP. The federal elections took place in the middle of their Presidency which meant that German leaders, and in particular, Klaus Kinkel, the Foreign

Minister and former FDP leader, were unable to concentrate fully on EU affairs. The Germans had indicated at the start of their Presidency that central and eastern Europe would be their top priority and they worked steadily, with strong Commission support, to achieve agreement on the "pre-accession strategy" at the Essen European Council. Apart from their traditional and expected concentration on central and eastern Europe, the Germans also provided for a wider dimension with a well-received Asia strategy paper which called for greater EU involvement in the Far East.

The debate in Germany about the IGC has been dominated by the Schäuble/Lamers paper on a "hard core" Europe. Published in September 1994, a month before the federal elections, the paper aroused considerable controversy and not a little anxiety in Germany and Europe. Although never adopted officially by the government, the proposals were given wide currency as they had been supported by the highest levels in the CDU. At present, the German position would seem to be more in favor of all member states proceeding to commitments entered into at the IGC, and to revert to the hard core idea only as a last resort.

German external policy will continue to be restrained by a number of factors including the burden of its history. This has a twofold impact. First is the general burden of the Nazi period and the reluctance to send the Bundeswehr to any country where the Wehrmacht was active. Second is the burden of the 1949-89 period which saw Germany achieve unrivalled prosperity as a result of no military engagement. For many Germans, not only on the left of the political spectrum, there seems no reason to change a tried and successful low-key foreign policy.

Another constraint is the restricted interpretation of the Karlsruhe decision of July 1994 on sending the Bundeswehr out of area. According to Kohl and Kinkel, such engage-ments will only take place under UN or OSCE authority and with full the support of the Bundestag. One should add to this the continued reluctance of public opinion to expose German soldiers to dangerous situations. (In this aspect the Germans are in good company with most Americans.) It is perhaps worth adding that Germany has no tradition of playing a global role. It never had a real empire (cf., UK and France) and since 1949 has been perfectly content to leave the U.S. to dominate its security policy.

For a variety of reasons, Germany will be reluctant to assume either the mantle of European leadership or to have to choose between the U.S. and France. Sitting on the fence may at times be uncomfortable, but it is the preferred German position. Thus Germany is in favor of widening *and* deepening the EU; of enlarging to the east *and* to the south; of enlarging NATO *and* seeking a strategic partnership with Russia; of strengthening WEU *and* NATO-but not increasing its defense budget. If and when Germany secures a permanent seat on the UN Security Council, attitudes may change, but probably very slowly. Germany will thus seek to continue its current successful mix of policies, to become only gradually involved in global affairs (preferably through the EU) and to avoid having to make hard choices.

The French Position.

The French have been consistently opposed to extending the community approach to CFSP. For the French, the Elysée is the center of decisionmaking in foreign and security policy. They have a completely different approach than the Germans to the concept of the nation-state. For the French (and the British) it is something positive: for the Germans something rather negative.

There is little doubt that the French have been the big losers as a result of the geopolitical changes since 1989. French discomfort at the possible consequences of German unification were obvious. Some have pointed to the marginalization of France, politically, strategically, and geographically. The EU is now looking east, where the main new markets are situated, rather than to the south, which is widely regarded as a trouble spot. France may still have its seat on the UN Security Council but Germany also looks set to join this club. France still has nuclear weapons, but what relevance are they in today's world?

French *angst* has been recognized in Bonn and Kohl has gone out of his way to assuage French concerns by consulting Paris on all important foreign policy issues. He has also made it clear that Bonn and Paris should coordinate their positions for the IGC.

In the aftermath of German unification and the recognition that the countries of central and eastern Europe were turning toward the EU in the expectation of membership, the French launched the idea of a European Confederation. It was never clear how this body would relate to the OSCE (then the CSCE), nor to the EU. President Havel led the attack on the French proposal, suggesting that it was a scarcely veiled device to postpone EU membership for the new democracies of central and eastern Europe.

The French proposal for a Stability Pact (basically pressing the central and east European states to resolve their minority problems) also met with initial skepticism in Europe but as the roundtables began to work, it was recognized that the mix of EU diplomatic pressure and carrots (more money for cross-border projects) was able to achieve results. The Stability Pact concluding conference held in Paris in March 1995 was generally welcomed as a useful exercise in preventive diplomacy.

The French Presidency also coincided with national elections which meant that French leaders could not devote their full attention to EU affairs. The Stability Pact was timed to conclude during their Presidency (a month before the elections!) Other priority areas included the Mediterranean and Rwanda, where the French (and Belgians) initially acted alone and then were supported, albeit with varying degrees of enthusiasm, by other member states.

The French debate on the IGC has been extremely bland as a result of the Presidential elections. It remains to be seen whether the new President will continue Mitterrand's general support for the European enterprise or whether he will seek to develop a more Gaullist approach. There are strong voices in France arguing for such an approach, whereas the supporters of closer European integration are conspicuous by their absence. In some areas (e.g., opposition to qualified majority voting in CFSP, opposition to increased powers for the European Parliament), the French will have the British as their (un)natural allies. On other issues (e.g., economic and monetary union) they will be seeking to maintain the German commitment.

The British Position.

John Major returned from Maastricht claiming "game, set and match" for the British, having successfully negotiated an opt-out on economic and monetary union and on social policy. He had also ensured that there would be a separate pillar structure, organized on inter-governmental lines, for CFSP and Justice/Home Affairs. Despite these "achievements," the British government almost tore itself apart during the ratification of the Maastricht Treaty. The divisions over Europe within the Conservative Party are such that the government's overriding objection at the IGC will be to refrain from accepting any proposal which could further deepen party divisions. Indeed Major is on record as stating that he will veto any change to the present institutional system.

The British Presidency (last half of 1992) was overshadowed by the dramatic and unsuccessful fight to keep the pound within the European Monetary System. The CFSP was not then in operation and the British were reluctant to take any initiatives in advance of the TEU's ratification. Since its entry into force on November 1, 1993, the British have spoken in favor of a strengthened CFSP but have not been prepared to countenance any significant changes to the operation of CFSP. Douglas Hurd has argued that CFSP requires a running-in period and that it is out of the question to move to majority voting.

In the spring of 1995 the British put forward a proposal designed to increase modestly the capabilities of the WEU. The proposal was received coolly by partners as it appeared to take a step back from the Maastricht text describing the WEU as an integral part of the development of the EU. The British have also been extremely cautious about any moves which they consider might tempt the U.S. to further disengage from Europe. At times their insistence on the preeminence of NATO seems more American than the U.S. position.

The British have made some attempts to improve their relations with both France and Germany. With France the main area of interest has been in the defense field, while with Germany, it has been the economic field. But London suffers a credibility gap in both Paris and Bonn for its failure to articulate a clear commitment to the goals of European integration.

Conclusion.

Jacques Delors used to pose three questions about foreign policy to member states of the EU: "What are our essential common interests? Are we prepared to act together to defend these interests? If so, with what resources?" These questions, to which the member states have given no adequate response, remain valid today and will become even more valid in light of subsequent enlargement of the Union.

No one doubts that developing a credible and effective CFSP will take time and will require familiarity, practice and confidence. Time is not on the Union's side, however, since the need for an effective CFSP, recognized by public opinion in the member states, is even greater now than it was at the time of Maastricht. The end of the Cold War and the collapse of the Soviet Union have been accompanied by the appearance of new risks to European security.

There can be no effective CFSP without the whole- hearted participation of all member states. The British (and the French) seem incapable of overcoming their ideological hostility to the community approach in foreign policy. They certainly have an argument concerning the sensitive issue of distribution of votes in the Council. But even if they were to receive a larger number of votes, it seems unlikely that they would agree to drop their veto in CFSP. Nor do they seem willing to accord the Commission a greater role in representing the EU to the outside world.

At present, the British and French governments take the view that only minor adjustments are required and that the CFSP must remain firmly on an inter-governmental basis. It must be doubtful, however, whether an enlarged EU with perhaps up to 25-30 member states can operate an effective CFSP purely on an inter-governmental basis. The danger is, as French Minister Lamassoure pointed out in March, that the EU would degenerate into the OSCE or League of Nations. Germany will thus have a key role to play in moves to strengthen the CFSP. Will it be content to join the Big Three and form a de facto 'directoire'? Or will it put itself at the head of the community camp? At some stage Germany will have to make a hard choice.

THE EUROPEAN UNION'S COMMON FOREIGN AND SECURITY POLICY RETROSPECTIVE ON THE FIRST EIGHTEEN MONTHS

Roy H. Ginsberg

Introduction.

Title V provisions for a Common Foreign and Security Policy (CFSP) of the Treaty on European Union (TEU) entered into force on November 1, 1993. Eighteen months later, what can be said of CFSP as a process of decision- making and a deliverer of goods? Is it a step up, or a step back, from its predecessor, European Political Cooperation (EPC)? Or, is there standstill? These questions are of particular moment as the European Union (EU) gears up for the next round of Treaty revisions in the 1996 Intergovernmental Conference (IGC). The IGC is slated to draft proposals which could improve the EU's decisionmaking and institutional structure ahead of EU enlargement to include many of the Central/Eastern European states. The last IGC-which ended in December 1991 in Maastricht-produced the TEU.

Whereas "maximalists" argue that there is an oppor- tunity to improve the functioning of the CFSP and to make headway in realizing the TEU's objective of a European Security and Defense Identity (ESDI), "minimalists" prefer to keep things as they are or to make only marginal changes. This paper is written just when the Reflection Group-representatives of the Foreign Ministers-is convening in June 1995 to prepare for the IGC. Four observations are offered at the outset.

First, there is a gap between what many of the TEU drafters sought to do when they authored Title V in 1991 and what has since transpired. Their vision of harnessing the resources and expertise of both the national governments engaged in political cooperation and the common bodies engaged in foreign economic diplomacy to form more consistent, rounded, and higher-profile joint actions has not materialized. Although some of the controversial issues of CFSP's functioning have been sorted out at least temporarily, many in the EU and the member governments remain very dissatisfied. Why the gap between vision and outcome?

Either not enough time has passed for the wrinkles to be ironed out of the provisions for joint CFSP actions and for closer links between the EU and its defense arm-the Western European Union (WEU)-or such provisions are flawed and in need of repair. The 1991 IGC which gave birth to CFSP itself was hastily conceived: many questions of procedure and substance were left unanswered. Haste made waste.

Current political conditions are less conducive to CFSP than they were in 1991. The Belgian Presidency was instrumental in putting CFSP into operation in late 1993, yet the Greek Presidency which followed won no such kudos. France and Germany held their EU Council Presidencies during national elections: needed attention and leadership were diverted from CFSP. CFSP's growth may also have been retarded as a result of the crisis of democratic legitimacy which has eroded public confidence in the EU and in the member governments since the Maastricht debates began.

Second, the anti-EU backbenchers now hold hostage the British Government's EU policy. Whereas in 1991 the government pushed for and received at Maastricht an inter-governmental pillar for CFSP, it now appears to take a much more narrow/strict (some would say obstructionist) view of CFSP's evolution. Are the British backpeddling? Have they lost interest in their own inter-governmental creation?

There is a split in the EU over how to develop CFSP and an absence of political will to overcome inevitable differences which accompany cooperation in such a sensitive sector. British ambivalence contrasts sharply with the support of Germany, the Commission, the Low Countries, and Ireland, among others. While the latter group was opposed to an inter-governmental approach in the first place, it has lent support to CFSP's implementation as originally envisaged: i.e., the better to relate the work of the EC bodies–the Commission and the Committee of Permanent Representatives (COREPER) aided by the Council Secretariat (called Pillar One in the TEU)–to that of the national capitals-based Political Directors who report to the Foreign Ministers (Pillar Two). Although generally keen to develop CFSP, the French have been known to resort to unilateral foreign policy action with more zest and frequency than most other members.

Third, with or without CFSP, the political/economic/ diplomatic influence of the EU will still be largely defined by the traditional Rome Treaty-based civilian actions of the European Community (EC). The EC still exists as one of the three pillars of the EU. CFSP/ESDI may in time enable the EU to back its economic diplomacy with a military capability; yet should they flounder, the EU will remain one of the two most influential actors in the global political economy (along with the United States).

Fourth, political will to make CFSP happen cannot be legislated. It should come as no great surprise that there is opposition to CFSP-after all, it is perceived to be a frontal assault on one of the last great bastions of state sovereignty. Whereas the IGC is widely expected to make only marginal changes in the functioning of CFSP, it is more likely to make headway in bringing the WEU and the EUROCORPS closer to the EU. The wars in Kuwait and ex-Yugoslavia-where the gap between European interests and capabilities was stunning-point to the need for the EU to move beyond its historical security constraints and from the rhetoric to the reality of a ESDI.

External stimuli have always played a large role in the EU's development as an international actor. It was never realistic to expect that the common market would forever remain isolated from the current of international politics. Indeed the quest to enhance the security of the common market goes back to the 1950s when the then Six came very close to achieving a defense community. Thus, whether or not ready, the EU is virtually condemned to act abroad. This means not just responding to external stimuli but representing and defending collective interests. Failure over time to develop and improve CFSP could demoralize, then contribute to the demise of the EU.

If the Fifteen are unable to agree as a whole to fix and revive CFSP at the 1996 IGC, a two or multiple speed CFSP may result. So long as the members either agree in general (or abstain) over a common position shared by a majority, some subset of the membership may wish to proceed with implementation, while others, less committed, may distance themselves without blocking "coalitions of the willing."

Primer.

The EU is an unorthodox international actor. Neither a state nor a conventional international organization, its foreign policy activities cannot be judged in traditional terms. EU foreign policy actions draw on two great traditions of cooperation:

• the integrationist tradition of the Rome Treaty based on the *acquis communautaire* (acquired EC laws and agreements), elements of supranational law, common institutions, habits of cooperation, and usage of qualified majority voting; and,

• the intergovernmentalist tradition of EPC, now CFSP, with its *acquis politique* (acquired political declarations/actions), legitimacy rooted in national interests and electorates, expertise drawn from the members' Foreign Ministries, and decisionmaking by consensus or unanimity.

Since its first incarnation in 1951, the EU has had a long and rich tradition of relations with many states, regions, and international organizations/regimes, and active involvement in a wide array of international commercial and political issues. Never a purely economic entity, yet never endowed with such state-like attributes as a common will and a military capability, still it has always been intimately linked to the security of Europe, the balance between East and West, and the functioning of the international political economy.

Common foreign economic diplomacy-the mainstay of today's EC civilian (nonmilitary) foreign policy-is rooted in the provisions of the Rome Treaty and based on qualified majority voting in some areas, consensus or unanimity in others. Examples of areas in the Treaty reserved for EC action include: enlargement, preaccession cooperation, association and preferential trade accords, tariff preferences, support for regional integration outside Europe, development/emergency aid, coordination of aid to Central/Eastern Europe on behalf of the Group-24, active support of human rights, bilateral political dialogues, multilateral trade liberalization negotiations, trade dispute settlement, economic/diplomatic sanctions, and diplomatic recognition.

Specific examples of recent Treaty-based foreign policy actions include mediation efforts in the war in ex-Yugoslavia and the establishment of the European Community Monitoring Mission (ECMM), withdrawing support for the new EU-Russian Partnership Accord over the Russian invasion of Chechnya, pressing President Yeltsin to accept a mission from the Organization of Security and Cooperation in Europe (OSCE) to maintain a permanent presence in Chechnya, working on a financial plan to close down the Chernobyl nuclear power plant, renewal of the financial protocol of the Lomé Convention, reviving relations with the Maghreb and the Mediterranean Basin, and developing ties with such new trade blocs as MERCOSUR-the Common Market of the South.

EPC, now CFSP, picks up where the Rome Treaty leaves off, given the latter's silence on foreign (political) policy and security. EPC started with foreign policy coordination in the 1970s and began considering the political-economic aspects of security in the 1980s. EPC had its strengths and weaknesses: it facilitated coordinated positions at the OSCE and toward the Arab-Israeli dispute, but it failed miserably to provide rapid responses to international crises (e.g., the run-up to and the outbreak of the U.S-Libyan conflict in 1986). EPC had neither an institutional nor a treaty base until 1987 when the Single European Act brought it closer to the EC and gave it a small secretariat.

Now in the 1990s the TEU opens up the door to a ESDI which years earlier was considered taboo. CFSP has the potential to be a major qualitative improvement over its predecessor. It explicitly links foreign and defense policy, raises the level of member governments' commitments to common action, and thus could go beyond the declaratory diplomacy which characterized but also limited the work of EPC.

While a main criticism of the CFSP is that the EU has yet to articulate a global and strategic vision for European foreign policy, there are a number of basic principles which are implicit in many of the EC/EU's foreign policy activities. Surely those principles are not uniformly applied to all foreign policy positions, but EU principles are as much at work in its actions as Canadian, German, or U.S. principles are at work in their actions.

The EU is a symbol of structural peace and reconciliation among ancient enemies. Championing human and civil rights, respect for the law, market and democratic reform, and the integration of other regional groups are corner- stones of EU foreign policies. These principles are inspired by the experiences of war, 19th century European liberalism, and the success of European regional integration in the last half of the 20th century.

The experience of digging out of the rubble of war to reclaim the dignity and rights of the individual and to achieve stability, prosperity, and security through regional integration is embedded in the shared Western European political culture of the post-war era. The EU is a magnet for nonmember European states and a model for other regions of the world. A prerequisite for membership in, and association with, the EU is that the applicant state must be a practicing democracy. This is a powerful inducement to change as evidenced by the dramatic democratic transitions in Greece, Spain, and Portugal. The EU's interregional policies, designed to support regional integration movements from Central and South America to Africa and from the Middle East to East Asia, testify to the wider legacy and example of European integration.

The gross violations of basic human rights by the Nazis and their collaborators before and during World War II have left an indelible mark on the EU members. As a result, human rights provisions are now regular features in most of the EU's foreign trade accords and the EU resorts to economic and diplomatic sanctions against foreign governments which violate basic human and civil rights (e.g., against Vietnam, Turkey, Rhodesia, Greece, and South Africa in the past and Nigeria, Sudan, Serbia, and Russia at present). A large share of common political positions and declarations are in response to violations of human rights and assaults on democratic government throughout the world.

EU foreign policy activity may be guided by a set of principles closely linked to the European project itself, but the EU is unable independently to defend those interests by military force-a contradiction with which the EU has had to grapple for over 40 years.

CFSP in Treaty Form.

The TEU created a new edifice-the European Union-supported by three pillars: the EC (Rome Treaty) formed Pillar One, EPC became CFSP and formed Pillar Two, and cooperation in justice and home affairs formed the basis for Pillar Three. Title V sought to develop high-profile joint actions which draw on the assets of the pillar system. The pillar system was designed to ensure consistency of actions across the various policy domains. To enhance EU security, the TEU designated the WEU to be its defense arm and charged the WEU with the task of devising plans to achieve that goal.

The potential for more rounded and consistent foreign policy across the pillars was given a boost by the Title V provisions which put COREPER in charge of preparing the meetings of the Council of Foreign Ministers. Previously, the Political Committee (comprised of Political Directors or senior staff from the members' Foreign Ministries) prepared for the EPC meetings of the Foreign Ministries outside the Rome Treaty framework. COREPER-a Brussels-based EC body of permanent representatives (or Ambassadors) from the member governments and serviced by the Council Secretariat-is well placed to link the foreign economic and political arms of the EU. Whereas COREPER has a panorama view of EU affairs, the Political Directors are far removed by virtue of their geographical location and political/national orientation. The extent to which the COREPER-Political Committee relationship has worked in ways consistent with the intentions of the most of the TEU founders is examined in the section on "CFSP Assessed."

Title V-as implemented under the Belgian Presidency-brought the old EPC secretariat inside the Council Secretariat, gave it a larger, more permanent staff, and a budget (EPC had a tiny staff seconded from the capitals and no budget). Title V highlights the notion of a joint action as the main medium for EU foreign policy. The topic of a joint action must be initially decided by the European Council on a unanimous basis but may then be implemented on the basis of qualified majority voting. Any member state, the Council, or the Commission may initiate a proposal for a joint action. The European Parliament (EP) is consulted at various stages of decisionmaking but otherwise the drafters chose to keep it at bay in the CFSP edifice. The extent to which the European Court of Justice (ECJ) has purview over an inter-governmental undertaking remains to be seen. Administrative expenses of joint actions were to come from existing budget lines in either the Commission or Council Secretariat. Operational expenses were to come from contributions from the member governments. What formula was to be used to achieve the latter and how the European Parliament was expected not to stick its nose in the former were left to the imagination.

CFSP in Practice.

On the basis of general guidelines issued by the European Council and pursuant to Article J.3 of the TEU, the Council decided on seven joint actions between November 1993-December 1994. This section briefly describes the basic actions and the next section offers a critical assessment.

Humanitarian Aid to Bosnia and the EU Civil Administration of Mostar. In the first CFSP joint action (November 8, 1993-Belgian Presidency), the Council decided, after having received the European Council's general guidelines (October 29), to increase its contributions for use by the U.N. High Commissioner for Refugees (HCR) and support the convoying of international aid in former Yugoslavia, particularly through the identification, restoration, and preservation of priority routes. Consultations were held between the EU (Presidency, Commission, the EC Monitoring Mission), the United Nations Protection Force (UNPROFOR), and the HCR.

In subsequent renewals and extensions, the Council included the EU's administration of the city of Mostar in this joint action in collaboration with the WEU. Financing came from either the EU budget (for operations) or from the member states on the basis of a GNP scale (for other costs). On June 13, 1994, the EU and WEU Presidents and the Bosnian Government agreed to a memorandum of understanding to establish the conditions for the EU administration of Mostar for a two-year period. Mr. Hans Koschnick was appointed Administrator. In October 1994 the Council allocated ECU 80 million to finance support for the EU Administration in 1995.

Dispatch of a Team of Observers for the Russian Parliamentary Elections. In the second CFSP joint action (November 9, 1993-Belgian Presidency), the Council decided, after having received the European Council's general guidelines (October 29), to support Russia's democratic transition by dispatching a team of observers to witness the Russian parliamentary elections of December 1993. The action was at the request of the Russian Government. The EU set up an elections monitoring unit in Moscow under the charge of the Presidency with full association of the Commission. The unit coordinated EU observers, coordinated with international organizations and other observers, and provided a link with Russian authorities. Administrative costs were borne by the Council budget; expenditures of observers were covered by the member governments who sent them.

Support for South Africa's Democratic Transition. In the third CFSP joint action (December 6, 1993-Belgian Presidency), the Council decided, after having received the European Council's general guidelines (October 29), to support South Africa's democratic transition by setting up a program of assistance to prepare for and monitor the first all-racial democratic elections. The EU electoral unit in South Africa assisted in the preparations for the elections in terms of offering advice, technical support and training, and support for nonpartisan voter education in advance of the election. Operational expenditures were drawn from the EC budget. Salaries and travel expenses incurred by the monitors were charged to the member states which sent them.

Sponsorship of an Inaugural Conference in Support of a Peace and Stability Pact. In the fourth CFSP joint action (December 20, 1993-Belgian Presidency), the Council decided, after having received the European Council's general guidelines (October 29), to hold a European conference to inaugurate a process by which ethnic and border disputes might be settled before they lead to war. Central and Eastern European states with border disputes and minority population problems are strongly encouraged by the EU to enter into bilateral compacts in which they agree to settle those disputes and protect those minorities' rights. Administrative costs associated with the holding of conferences were charged to the Council budget.

The inaugural conference was held in Paris on May 26-27, 1994. Delegates from 52 OSCE states attended as did representatives from other European and international organizations. The conference adopted conclusions setting out the aims and principles and operational arrangements for the establishment of regional roundtables. The EU declared its readiness to play an active role in bilateral talks and regional roundtables and make available appropriate aid. The agreements which come of the talks will be entrusted to OSCE. The OSCE will be asked to evaluate and monitor the implementation of the accords and the commitments made in them. Implicit in the joint action is how the lure of EU membership will catalyze Central/ Eastern European states, all of whom seek to join, to sign on to the pact. The historic treaty signed by Slovakia and Hungary in 1995 testifies to the success of the EU action.

Support for Middle East Peace. In the fifth CFSP joint action, the Council decided (April 19, 1994–Greek Presidency), after having received the European Council's general guidelines (October 29, 1993), to support the Middle East peace process by monitoring the settlements in the Occupied Territories, working to lift the Arab boycott of Israel, supporting the organization of an international economic conference on infrastructure projects in the region, supporting a new EU-Israel agreement, partici-pating in a future temporary international presence in the Occupied Territories as provided for in UN Security Council Resolution 904, helping to organize and monitor elections in Gaza and the West Bank, and supporting the new Palestinian Police Force. The financing of this joint action was not elaborated and was left to a future Council decision.

Support for the Renewal of the NNPT. In the sixth CFSP joint action, the Council decided (July 25, 1994–German Presidency), after having received the European Council's general guidelines (June 25, 1994), to strengthen the nuclear nonproliferation system by promoting the universality of the Nuclear Nonproliferation Treaty (NNPT) and by extending it indefinitely and unconditionally. The action includes EU approaches to states not yet party to the NNPT with offers to assist them with the decision to accede and with establishing procedures required for meeting Treaty obligations.

Control of Exports of Dual-Use Goods. In the seventh CFSP joint action, the Council decided (December 19, 1994–German Presidency), after having received the European Council's general guidelines (June 25, 1994), to establish a list of third country destinations to which the EC's new regime for the control of exports of dual-use goods (goods which can be used for both civil and military purposes) may be restricted.

CFSP Assessed.

Although small in number, the seven joint actions to date provide at least some empirical evidence with which to begin to assess how CFSP has worked in practice. Member governments took less ambitious actions at first to ensure success and to build public support. The joint actions were kept fairly low-key in part because they were designed as much for effect as for internal consensus-building. Over time, as confidence increases, joint actions may become more ambitious, but for now the premium has been on the "inward development" aspects over the outward ones. Five problem areas are identified for particular attention because, left neglected, they unnecessarily diminish CFSP.

Definition of Joint Action. Title V elaborates on the process of making joint actions, but offers no definition of what a joint action is. Is it joint among the 15 members or is it joint between the 15 members operating in CFSP on the one hand and the EC operating under the Rome Treaty on the other? The act of defining may have eluded the Maastricht negotiators because of the difficulty of reaching consensus among the member governments over such a sensitive matter, but if the member governments cannot agree to a definition of a joint action, it then boggles the mind to envisage the practice of joint action. A definition will help clarify the roles of the different pillars and demystify CFSP for European citizens-a goal worthy of the Reflection Group's consideration as it prepares for the next IGC.

Financing. With each of the joint actions which carried financial obligations, there were divisive debates. No one wanted to pay for joint actions. Title V does not create a CFSP budget. Pillar Two, the essence of intergovernmental cooperation, for all intents and purposes "raids" Pillar One's budget. Pillar One constitutes the entire EC budget, so it is rich in resources. The problem is that those resources have been approved by the European Parliament, audited by the Court of Auditors, and subject to the legal purview of the European Court of Justice. All three bodies belong to the EC in Pillar One.

Pillar Two depends completely on the Council Secretariat (a communitarian body) for institutional support and on the budget of the Commission or Council Secretariat to fund the administrative costs of joint actions. Article J.11 of the TEU stipulates that the administrative costs of CFSP joint actions may be charged to the EC budget and that the Council shall decide whether or not to charge the EC budget or the member governments for operational expenditures associated with joint actions. No guidance was offered as to how member governments would be assessed contributions. The Council has subsequently determined that contributions will be based on a GNP scale.

There can be no CFSP without a budget. Member governments are loathe to pay for joint actions–many are willing to siphon off funds already allocated to EC foreign aid programs under Pillar One. There are two problems with this stopgap measure.

First, since the Council has not codified the rules of financing joint actions, since many of the member governments do not have CFSP budget lines, and since the Commission and Council Secretariat have limited CFSP budgets, as each new joint action is proposed there will be a debate over how it is to be financed. This is hardly desirable in terms of the speed necessary to adopt joint actions which are in response to international crises. Additionally, if Pillar Two raids Pillar One's resources for the purposes of financing CFSP joint actions, then there are a number of legal and political problems which the Reflection Group will want to note. The three EC institu-tions with Rome Treaty mandates over spending and programs have been locked out of CFSP decisionmaking by the TEU drafters and the Foreign Ministers. The use of EC resources by a non-EC body infringes on the legal rights of EC bodies. How can EC funds be spent without proper safeguards, oversight, and accountability?

The British, who do not want Pillar One to "contaminate" Pillar Two, are also quick to shy away from funding of CFSP joint actions from national budgets. If the British accept Pillar One financing of Pillar Two actions, they will, in effect, be accepting the interpillar vision of CFSP they have publicly opposed.

Second, there is no such thing as a strictly intergovernmental framework for CFSP. For CFSP to work, it has to draw on the expertise, resources, continuity, stability, and memory of the EC institutions. An interpillar approach to CFSP means that when EC money is being spent and EC staff is being employed in the service of Pillar Two, the EC bodies must be able to fulfill their consti-tutional responsibilities. If the governments want CFSP to be divorced from the EC, they will have to staff and fund joint actions independently of the EC.

Institutions and Interpillar Relations. The pillar system is divisive. Every twist and turn in the development of CFSP has been a virtual battleground for the integrationists (or maximalists) and the inter-governmentalists (minimalists). This was not the vision of the majority of the TEU drafters. Their concept of a European Union was to create a single institutional framework to draw on both traditions of European cooperation. The Permanent Representatives sitting in COREPER were designated to be the liaison between the EC and CFSP and to coordinate EC and CFSP actions. Whereas in the past the Political Directors sitting in the Political Committee prepared EPC meetings of the Foreign Ministers (and hoped to retain that privilege), COREPER was charged by Title V to perform this important function. As mentioned, COREPER is uniquely situated to ensure EC-CFSP or interpillar consistency because it is a body which serves both the EC under the Rome Treaty and the national governments as Ambassadors.

Although the Political Committee must now pass its reports and agenda items through COREPER, this has apparently not diminished the Political Directors' impact on CFSP. Indeed, the Political Committee has remained more powerful and resilient to change than many TEU founders envisaged. Since COREPER is spread too thin simply covering the complexity of EC business, it must defer to the Political Committee's foreign policy advice and expertise. By appealing directly to their Foreign Ministers, there is ample room for the Political Directors to circumvent COREPER's new role. Since Political Directors work for national Foreign Ministers, they cannot be expected to play the role of ensuring interpillar consistency. Simply put, Political Directors are responsive to political administrations who in turn serve party and national interests. While representing national interests in Brussels, the Permanent Repre- sentatives work daily on European issues in a setting which demands sensitivity to reach common positions. Only COREPER can do this. The COREPER-Political Committee relationship encapsulates the tug of war between contending approaches to EU decisionmaking. The future of CFSP may well depend on how the two bodies work out a *modus operandi*.

The Commission is caught between a rock and a hard place. It was granted the right of initiative in Pillar Two long denied to it when it was associated loosely with the old EPC. So far it has not chosen to exercise that right. It is concerned that if it fully engages in the procedures of Pillar Two, its independence, resources, and competencies under the Rome Treaty will be eroded. It fears the "intergovernment- alization" of Pillar One by Pillar Two. Yet it wants to play a constructive role. It has reorganized itself to bolster its foreign policy staff of experts in anticipation of playing a critical role in CFSP. Only time will tell how the Commission manages to balance EC and CFSP foreign relations without undermining its independence and competencies under the Rome Treaty. The Commission is well situated to ensure that CFSP actions are consistent with EC ones.

The Council Secretariat, now home to the old EPC operations, has been slow to fully integrate the culture of inter-governmental political cooperation with the culture of the permanent staff and their communitarian way of doing things. The new CFSP Directorate has been slow to take shape. Its size—about 25 professional staffers (half seconded from the Foreign Ministries for 5-year periods and half permanent)–will remain small relative to the 250 or so professionals staffing the Commission's international operations and thus may constrict its ability to provide timely forward analyses. Nonetheless, the CFSP staff will have more permanence and resources than did its predecessor.

The EP got the short end of the stick in the CFSP apparatus. Parliament wants CFSP to be financed from the EU budget so that it may exercise its full powers with regard to approving budgets for and scrutinizing expenditures of joint actions. A number of Foreign Ministers tend on the whole to reject such parliamentary intrusion. A CFSP which lacks democratic legitimacy with, and accountability to, the European electorate will be undercut by the lack of popular support. The 1996 IGC ought to give the EP the right to exercise its powers over any CFSP expenditures which are drawn from EC resources. In exchange for its place in the CFSP edifice, Parliament may be willing to propose that a permanent portion of the Commission's yearly budget include a CFSP reserve.

The WEU has made some progress in moving closer to the EU, but the pace of WEU-EU (as well as WEU-NATO) cooperation is much slower than many of the TEU founders had envisaged. The WEU headquarters has moved from London to Brussels and the WEU Presidential term of one year has been reduced to 6 months to complement the EC Council Presidency. There is an attempt to have the EC Council Presidency coincide with the WEU Council Presidency to the extent possible. The WEU has established a planning cell, identified areas in which it can make a contribution to enhancing European security, and beefed up its intelligence and research capabilities. Despite these and other adjustments and innovations (e.g., WEU-EU collaboration in Mostar and expansion of the WEU to include additional EU members as either full or associated members), the slowness with which the member governments have moved to develop WEU-EU ties reveals reservations some EU member governments have over developing the ESDI. It bodes well for the future of the EU as a security actor that in January 1994 the NATO Council endorsed ESDI, CFSP, the WEU as the EU's defense arm and as the strengthened European pillar of NATO, and the notion of a Combined Joint Task Force (to enable the WEU to take military action using NATO assets). Still, much of the above remains in the planning stage and little substantive action has followed.

Decisionmaking. Title V opened the door to qualified majority voting (QMV) in the implementation of joint actions, but to date all actions have been decided on the basis of consensus. This is due no doubt to the fear of beginning a precedent. After all, what most clearly differen- tiates the integrationist from the inter-governmentalist approach is voting method: continued use of unanimity (consensus), even where the TEU opens the door to QMV, ensures the triumph of inter-governmentalism and the sovereignty of the states. The eventual introduction of QMV in the implementation of joint actions may help "break the ice." However, there is no substitute for the opportunity to use QMV in the European Council when the Heads of Government make the initial commitment to act in tandem and lay down the broad guidelines for the Council (of Foreign Ministers) to implement.

A CFSP which remains based on unanimity lacks the flexibility which a group of 15 states needs in dealing with the outside world. Increased use of abstention may help get around the requirement of unanimity. "Consensus minus one" could help the EU take international action over the objections of one member government. A two- or multiple-speed CFSP may permit coalitions of the willing to take common action so long as the membership as a whole- or a qualified majority or a consensus minus-either supports (or does not oppose) a general framework for such action.

Lastly, since QMV as currently devised gives more weight to the smaller states relative to the largest ones and given the future growth of the EU to include many new small states, the Reflection Group will likely recommend a new QMV formula. A new formula would retain QMV, and thus not eliminate the influence of smaller states, but give the four most powerful states (United Kingdom, France, Germany, and Italy) a heavier weighing to take into account population size. There is no hope for increased usage of QMV unless it is revised to accommodate the big states, without whom there can be no CFSP. At the same time, a new QMV formula which grossly reduces the influence of the smaller states threatens to erode the very foundations of the EU-foundations which respect the rightful place of all states in the European project.

The Scope of Joint Actions to Date. Based on the experience to date, the concept of joint action may be too much of a straitjacket to be useful. For example, each time a joint action is proposed and the philosophical, budgetary, and interpillar implications are assessed, old wounds are opened between the minimalist-inter-governmentalists and the maximalist-integrationists. Fights occur not over the value of action but over the means. The competition and mistrust which exist between Pillars One and Two have stymied the evolution of CFSP.

The joint action to convoy humanitarian aid in ex-Yugoslavia would probably have been achieved under the old EPC. However, the decision to set up a civil admin- istration in Mostar with the aid of the WEU does represent a step up from EPC. How the WEU and EU cooperate in Mostar may affect the pace of their future union. Despite wishes to the contrary, the EU cannot walk away from the Balkans, and the Mostar action represents a new phase in the development of its foreign policy. The action to dispatch a team of election observers to Russia in some respects diminishes rather than validates CFSP. However, it was designed more for the inward development aspect of CFSP-to build inner confidence in the use of joint action-than to have important external effects. After all, nongovernmental organizations are perhaps better suited to handle election monitoring given the host of other foreign policy actions worthy of the EU's attention.

The South African action was different from the Russian one. The EU spent considerable time and resources in South Africa educating people and carefully preparing them for the democratic transition. It was more than a mere monitoring mission. It was a step up from EPC but yet modest enough so that the EC could claim a CFSP success. The Peace and Stability Pact Conference and follow-up was a major success for CFSP. Having experienced the failure of its mediation efforts in ex-Yugoslavia and having failed to better prepare for, indeed seek to preempt, the inevitability of ethnic strife in the post-Tito period, the EU sought to use a new approach: i.e., to use preventative diplomacy. It proceeded to work closely with states who have border disputes or minority problems by offering rewards (EU membership) in exchange for confidence-building contracts stabilizing border regions and guaranteeing the rights of ethnic minorities in foreign lands. The joint action concerning the Middle East peace process was an example of the EU looking for something constructive to do in this volatile region. Much of what is in this joint action has already been done or could have been done by the EC in conjunction with the old EPC. Support for renewal of the NNPT and for limits of exports of dual-use goods are security-type actions which may pave the way for the future ESDI but are still rather modest in scope.

The number of joint actions remains low. While some of the actions would have been undertaken under the pre-CFSP regime, others did add value to the old EPC and bode well for the future. As a means to develop CFSP, the use of joint action may end up diminishing rather than elevating common European positions. CFSP is more than joint actions: besides the requisite political will to act together, it includes common positions and declarations and the many ways in which political cooperation and economic diplomacy interact to form more consistent and effective "joint EC-CFSP joint actions."

CFSP and the Next Intergovernmental Conference.

What are some of the likely outcomes of the IGC? Minimalists call for only changes at the margins-reforming QMV to take into account national population (British view), strengthening the Council Secretariat CFSP Directorate to handle CFSP (French view), and bringing the WEU closer to, but not necessarily inside, the EU by possibly creating a fourth pillar (British and Danish view). Maximalists call for permanent CFSP budget lines for the Commission, the Council Secretariat, and the member governments; the EC bodies to assume their legal right of purview over CFSP spending drawn from the EC budget; increased usage of modified QMV in the implementation of joint action; introduction of modified QMV in the initial adoption of the principle of a joint action; and reexamination of the COREPER-Political Committee relationship to determine how best to manage the CFSP agenda and to ensure interpillar consistency. Some maximalists go as far as to press for the integration of the defense industry into the common market to create the conditions for harmonized product standards and thus hasten the coming of a ESDI.

The EU's future enlargement, which could double its membership, is a strong possibility. Decisionmaking will become even more difficult than it is now. One antidote is to introduce modified QMV into all CFSP decisionmaking. Another antidote is to accept a two- or multiple-speed CFSP as an unfortunate but necessary concomitant of an enlarged Union. This would require a complicated formula in which a minority of members would agree not to block the wishes of the majority and would not participate in the implementation of an action. The precedents for such a scenario come from other areas of the EU: monetary and social integration where members agree to move at different speeds within the same general direction. In the end, the IGC, which may last 2 or more years, will likely produce outcomes straddling the fault lines of the minimalists and the maximalists.

THE IMPORTANCE OF CFSP FOR GERMAN FOREIGN POLICY

Josef Janning

Introduction.

To develop a coherent Common Foreign and Security Policy (CFSP) has been and remains of principal interest to Germany's European policy. This is partly due to external pressures on the European Union (EU) as perceived in Germany and partly due to internal preferences and constraints on the country's role in Europe and beyond. Among the motives and interests governing this policy, three arguments deserve closer attention. First is the functional argument, i.e., the adaptation of the Union's framework to the post-1989 perspective of European integration. Second is the solidarity argument, i.e., the interest in developing the EU's partnership quality. And third is the alliance argument, i.e., the ability of Germany fully to participate in the preservation of European security and defense.

Negotiating CFSP at Maastricht: Interests and Achievements in a German Perspective.

In close, but not full cooperation with France, Germany was among the key proponents of increasing European Political Cooperation into a foreign and security policy framework beyond the inter-governmental level. The Franco-German initiatives in the preparation of the Maastricht Treaty drove the negotiations in 1990 and 1991. As seen from Bonn, Political Union was to be the wished for twin sister of Monetary Union; a quid pro quo approach to the French strategy of strengthening the ties that hold member states together beyond the East-West conflict. At the time, the new demands on Germany's ability to contribute to the security and defense of the West and of western interests had already become a political issue with the Gulf War, the Kurdish-Turkish issue, the break-up of Yugoslavia and other variants of the out-of-area debate. In the European theater, concerns about the impact of German unification for the balance of the new Europe opened the window for a significant advancement in the field of foreign and security policy.

Building on the French determination to strengthen the ties of integration, the German government was able decisively to shape this process of deepening. Monetary Union was devised mostly along the German preferences helped by the sensible management of Jacques Delors except for one issue of principle nature in the German politico-academic debate: European Monetary Union (EMU) implementation would adhere to objective criteria but would also follow a defined time-table that could run counter to the German "Kronungsthese" according to which the EMU should be the ultimate reward to states for achieving coherence in monetary and fiscal stability.

The inclusion of foreign policy and security policies into the deepening of the European integration was based on a range of motives and interests among which three were probably most important:

• the risk of a falling apart of the foreign policy priorities and orientations as a result of the recasting of Europe and a tendency of de-solidarization under the new conditions among essential member-states;

• the interest to maintain and develop an integrated framework for security and defense issues, which could also adequately reflect the security challenges and the growing political responsibility of the West Europeans for the organization of their own security; and,

• the perception of the emergence of new risks and challenges to the stability of the political, economic and social systems in Western Europe, their territorial integrity and normative quality that would not be or insufficiently be protected through the old instruments.

In the negotiations, these motives were not shared by all of the member-states. For France and Germany, however, all of these issues were of special importance. Based on their respective national interests, both states articulated an interest to integrate the other into a common framework. The balance sheet on Political Union, namely on CFSP, indicates a lower leverage of Germany and France than could have been expected at the outset of the negotiations. On the one hand, the Franco-German position, by and large, prevailed both in the EU and within NATO: the development of foreign policy making, security and defense in Western Europe was to be conceived as complementary to the other areas of European integration and this result could not be achieved through the partial identity of the actors in different organizations alone. The provisions on a CFSP continue the experimental and pragmatic approach of integration policies since the 1970s.

In perspective, the provisions sketch out the option of a security union in which the Western European Union (WEU) organizes a common and potentially integrated defense under the roof of the European Union. However incremental, the Maastricht Treaty clarified the Union's position in two directions:

• The deepening of European integration will not proceed on the basis of a civilian power that abstains from the conflicts in international politics.

• Within the future development of the Atlantic Alliance, the "European Pillar" would be made up by a WEU which is an integral part of the European Union. Thus, an old debate within NATO had been settled from the European side. In addition, the West Europeans had offered a complementary model for both their continuing interest in NATO and the necessities of integration within the EC.

Some of the Franco-German proposals were not realized, namely in the sector of foreign policy. Six issues from the position papers were not or were inadequately translated into treaty language:

• The assignment of specific tasks to the CFSP process, including the relations to the eastern and southern neighborhood of the EU, transatlantic relations, CSCE and the UN;

• A common policy on arms control and arms exports, non-proliferation and arms procurement;

• The ability of the Union to participate in peacekeeping and peace-enforcement beyond the UN peacekeeping scheme;

• The linkage of the Union to multilateral and integrated defense structures;

• A clear assignment of the WEU to act as the EU's European pillar within NATO; and,

• The integration of development policies and development assistance into the CFSP framework.

The list reflects the reluctance of other member states to begin CFSP with substantive assignments but it also indicates the limits of Franco-German cooperation. As government sources in Bonn have occasionally hinted, the German side was prepared to move far ahead in integrating its foreign policy and defense resources; but could not win full support from Paris. After a phase of pressing for more integration in 1990, French policy became less explicit in the actual negotiations. Illustrative of the policy style inside the "axis," most of the subsequent texts were drafted in Bonn and issued in Paris.

The Functional Argument: Ostpolitik and CFSP.

Since the early steps of European integration in the 1950s, German European policy has looked upon the process as being functional to German foreign policymaking. From Adenauer's strategy of seizing sovereignty in order to regain it to Helmut Kohl's approach to a European Germany, administrations have used the integration framework for the articulation of German interests. Among the multi- lateral settings, the EC/EU was probably most responsive to Germany's needs and its policy style. The EC's implicit values were closer to the internationalist spirit of the Federal Republic's diplomacy, depicted ironically as a form of "Machtvergessenheit" ("power forgetfulness") by Hans-Peter Schwarz in 1985.

Beyond such behavioral patterns, the conduciveness of integration to German interests was put to a new test after 1989. From the German point of view, the grand political project of the coming decade will be to realize the integration of the European democracies on the terms of the European Union. In this context, CFSP is seen as the vehicle to tackle the far-reaching foreign policy implications of the enlargement process–from the management of relations with Russia and the Russian-controlled parts of the CIS, to the trade and subsidies related aspects of integrating "tiger economies" or the balancing of security concerns of the South and the East of the expanded European Union.

Germany's particular interest in adapting the EU framework to its own perspective is evident. The prospective members are mostly direct neighbors of Germany or close neighbors to these countries, their trade is focused on the attractive German market, and migratory flows are centered on Germany. Bearing the investment patterns and the anticipated effects of market integration for East Central Europe in mind, Germany probably has the strongest interests and position in the region. Over- shadowed by the burden of history in its various bilateral relationships, German politics and business are often confronted with positions and demands from these countries that could neither be met nor rejected without political or fiscal harm. In all of these cases, applying the integration framework to these issues would help the German position, be it on property rights or labor mobility, security concerns or, simply, communication styles in the day-to-day management of bilateral affairs. European norms and procedures, demands or interferences are not subject to a hegemonic suspense–yet.

In addition to this, European integration is functional to German interests in another important dimension. For a number of reasons, Germany does not want to choose between East and West and thus has no interest in conducting its relations with the East in a different mode than those with the West. Without integrating the new democracies into the Union, however, such a difference could hardly be avoided, given the asymmetry between Europe's largest population and economy and its East Central European neighbors. Each of the historic German Sonderwege (special ways) has a reflex of the geopolitical position of the country in the center of Europe. In this sense, enlarging the Union eastwards offers a way out of geopolitical determinism–in a European Union of 20 or 25, there is no Mittellage (middle position) for Germany in the old sense of the word. Attached to these considerations is the issue of balance of power and counterbalancing strategies. Enlarging the EU would not make such strategies altogether impossible, but could contribute to their taming.

With this centrality of Eastern enlargement in mind, the reform interests of Germany's European policy with regard to CFSP aim at a strengthening of the Union's international position–if only to be able to communicate with Russia on a proper basis. Furthermore, the Union should prepare to extend forms of security assurances to those incoming members that are not covered by other institutions–a second or maybe even third best alternative but one that could be disregarded if the interest in NATO enlargement were to be credible.

Finally, reforms should reflect the change in the relationship between member states and European institutions. The ratification of Maastricht signalled that the linear approach to European integration, leading toward the emergence of a European federal state, had been surpassed by the peaceful revolutions. For the future, European politics should seek to make effective use of the reappearing national resources and power of its members. Now that a purely communitarian approach to CFSP (which had enjoyed some sympathy in Germany prior to the Maastricht treaty) is out of the question, majority voting and community procedures are hardly to be expected. Therefore, a CFSP reform should allow for greater flexibility to permit "coalitions of the willing" or "coalitions for action." The German preference may rather be on those options that promise greater ability to act than on those whose principal merit is institutional progress.

The Solidarity Argument: Europe as a Power in the Making.

To look at CFSP as a vehicle for the assumption of partnership quality represents a special case of addressing the external implications of the Union's internal devel-opment and its changing environment. The completion of the internal market program has put flesh on the implicit argument in favor of integration as a process involving the creation of a community of destiny that does not stop at the level of mutual economic benefits. In consequence, the almost unrestricted opening of markets is accompanied by the perception that the external interests, risk assessments and security concerns of one member are shared by all other partners beyond the level of "mutual recognition"; to apply a term from the internal market linguistics.

However deeply the collapse of the Soviet Union has changed those perceptions and facts, Europe remains the most exposed and highly vulnerable region in world affairs. It directly neighbors two zones of potential instability and threat and it is located on the border of major civilizations which face large challenges, even if a clash among them may not become reality. Thus, the EU could be confronted with conflicts that will bring with them economic losses, migratory waves, a new quality of terrorism and blackmail (from boycott or environmental hazards to non-conventional weapons) and it has prototypes of the new aggressions and low-intensity conflicts in its neighborhood. Just as the other centers of the former First World (but more directly so), European states feel the implications of the known and newly emerging "global issues" arising from disruptions of the earth's ecological, demographic and social balances. At the same time, the EU has moved into the need for policies of scale. Most visibly in the sectors of trade and aid, decisions taken by the EU and its members affect third parties decisively. These are the factors that ground Germany's interest in developing the European Union's capacity to act on the global scale. As a key country of the union, much of Germany's own world political interests center around the stability interests of the EU as such and therefore require effective policymaking at the union level in order to optimize the ability to articulate and protect the collective as well as the embedded national interests of its members.

Clearly, the range of Germany's interests that are to be pursued via the EC/EU framework has expanded beyond securing the country's position in the West, its acceptance as a democratic state, or the preservation of an environment conducive to special German interests such as the German option for unification. For the future, EU foreign policy-making should thus be conducive to the new items on Germany's agenda—from competitiveness vis-à-vis Asia to the establishment of global trade and finance schemes, from development policies to global stability management, from partnership with Russia on an equal footing to the strengthening of transatlantic relations with the United States. On many of these issues Germany's potential and influence may be essential to the formulation of a European response, but in all of them the country lacks the critical mass to respond by its own means only.

Beyond the bloc structure, Germany's centrality to other actors is bound to change. In the multi-layered system of the 1990s there exists no clearly defined central front. The critical mass for the articulation of Germany's interests now rests within the institutions of European integration and its organization has become the resource for partnership relations with the world powers. With regard to transatlantic relations, the perspective of "partners in leadership" in Western affairs will require an EU capable of action rather than the added-up foreign policy ("zusammengesetzte Aussenpolitik," as Rummel has called it) of the EPC-type. Germany should be among those leading the way into a partnership of this sort given her interests in attracting the United States to Europe under the conditions of the new era.

In terms of CFSP reform, the emergence of the EU as a global actor seems to be too much of a challenge to be realized easily. Rather, the process to be started in 1996 will be confined to gradual and careful advances. Of immediate concern in this direction is the advancement of an EU planning capacity through a combined infrastructure at the EU-level and forms of direct access to the resources of the national foreign policy administrations (e.g., in the form of a diplomatic double-hatting). The link between the EU's commercial power and its security components needs to be stronger and more visible. Political leadership and personalization of policies should not be limited to the top bureaucratic level but could be expressed through a CFSP-presidency of one member state within a reformed troika system.

The Alliance Argument: The Role of CFSP and WEU in the Defense of Europe.

To the present day, Germany's armed forces are integrated into the military structure of NATO to a higher degree than any of her neighbors. In the public awareness, military spending and the maintenance of Western Europe's largest conventional army has been a direct function of the Soviet threat and was almost exclusively legitimized by the existence of the Warsaw Pact. At no time has the acceptance of armed forces for the "purposes of greatness" in Germany been lower than in the past decades and assignments outside of the central front scenario hardly ever have been debated. Both of these formative factors of the German defense posture have been put to question in the aftermath of the peaceful revolutions in Eastern Europe. Among NATO's European members, the degree of renationalization and unilateral disarmament has surpassed the expectations of the early 1990s, the southern, south-eastern and the Baltic flank have been seriously weakened; and the pressures on the fiscal burdens of defense have multiplied. At the same time, the emergence of new conflicts and war in Europe as well as the applicability of conventional forces to their control have found Germany ill prepared–in legal, structural and mental terms.

Germany is least able to react to those challenges that are most likely to require the use of military force in almost all of the forms these actions may take. A gap between the capabilities and the interests has opened up that harms Germany's political position and role. The emergence of zones of lesser security in East Central Europe affects the German interest in the stability of the region. The constraints on the use of the German armed forces minimize the German influence in conflict management, as well as Germany's role in the new military cooperation schemes on the continent. And, the fragmentation of arms procurement structures imposes a rising burden on the federal budget already stressed by the costs of unification, and the weakness of a credible European framework to integrate Germany's defense resources feeds public skepticism and resentment.

The renationalization of defense structures and the multilateralization of military action on the basis of voluntary national contributions tend to cement the German problem. Just as the country seeks to avoid a choice between East and West, it seems yet unprepared to choose between defense integration and military contributions to actions in a multilateral setting. Equally unattractive appears the choice between acting under these circumstances and not acting at all. The German preference is clearly directed toward collective forms of a permanent rather than an ad hoc-nature. On the basis of collective institutions, participation in multilateral activities seems manageable in the future. Germany has no interest in maintaining the current trap of not fully being able to act in solidarity. Given the patterns of change within NATO, collective frameworks should build on the defense of Europe's territorial integrity (which in a German perspective is still a valuable and necessary collective task); should include collective risk assessment and contingency planning; provide mandating power for action; share reconnaissance, C^3I and airlift capabilities; and, be accountable to the European pillar of the Western alliance. NATO should be understood as an alliance of the democracies of Europe and North America rather than as a defense pact of the "old" West.

Current CFSP and its future development have a crucial role in Germany's thinking. It is the link between the soft power of the EU and the emerging resources of WEU, as well as an anchor for the new elements of defense integration in the bi- and multi-national military units that could compensate for Germany's past symbiosis of German and allied forces. Thus, the time for a common defense policy and a common defense seems to be nearer than the Maastricht Treaty on European Union has stated. CFSP reform along these lines should seek to turn the implicit security guarantee of EU-membership into an explicit one by introducing a solidarity clause of the type of NATO's or WEU's Article V to the treaty, assigning the WEU clearly to the security of the union and establishing a link to the EUROCORPS, including the other multinational units existing and under preparation. Also, such an arrangement of responsibilities and institutional settings would make more plausible a binary relationship between the EU and the United States inside and outside the larger alliance of democracies.

Conclusion.

In sum, the centrality of the CFSP process to Germany and German foreign and security policy will be articulated in the upcoming negotiations. This should not be read as an almost unrestricted push on the part of the German government for major advances-negotiators have become rather careful if not timid in light of the ratification experience of the Maastricht Treaty. It should also not be misread as a government policy position which oscillates between integrationist proposals and the attraction of inter-governmental and extra-EU offerings. It rather suggests a rationale for a reform perspective of the CFSP of the EU that is compatible with, and conducive to, the interests and preferences that may be attributed to the united Germany in the 1990s.

ENDNOTES

1. The views expressed are personal and do not commit the European Commission in any way.

2. This is the logical path which two senior officials from the Auswärtiges Amt correctly identified in an article in the Frankfurter Allgemeine on 30 March 1995.

www.ingramcontent.com/pod-product-compliance
Lightning Source LLC
Chambersburg PA
CBHW080106010626
45794CB00015B/3295